Edging Gradually

Towards Oblivion

Original Poetry

By

Aisla Houghton-Foster

Published in Liverpool
by Wi-Fi Butterfly Publications

Edging Gradually Towards Oblivion

Aisla Houghton-Foster
& Wi-Fi Butterfly Publications
ahfwrites@gmail.com
ahfwrites.com

ISBN: 979 8 80117 523 2

Cover Photograph by Helen Houghton-Foster.
Cover Design by Aisla Houghton-Foster.

First Printing Edition 2022.
Published by Wi-Fi Butterfly Publications,
c/o. Amazon KDP.

For Helen,
my rock, my anchor,
my sensible-signpost!

Contents

Introduction

The following collection of poetry is going to be a triggering experience for you.

This might sound like it comes out of nowhere. How could you have expected such a thing - especially since the title is so cheery and happy and carefree?! I know right?

Joking aside, many of the poems in this collection are deeply personal for me and the result is that many explore dark and difficult themes. They stem from the depths of my mind, plagued as it is with sadness, frustration, anger, despair and loneliness. Many years of mental health difficulties, transition-related issues and stresses of various sorts have inspired what you are going to read in so many different ways.

Yet something to keep in mind as you read – and indeed, as you hopefully pick up on my humour and sense of irony – I am not simply a miserable bitch!

While the content of this work is often heavy and hard to think about, I hope that you are able to also see the funny side and engage in the levity that all to often is a coping mechanism for the challenges people like me face.

This will no doubt be clear from the minute you start reading *Vortex* on page one!

<u>Poetry and Me</u>

I have been writing poetry since I was a child and I have been around poetry for even longer.

My mum used to read poetry to me before I was even born, as well as being a very poetic and creative person herself. Both she and my dad were huge fans of poetry and literature more generally, and I was fortunate to grow up in a household that was filled with poetry books. Indeed, my dad, who died of a brain tumour when I was fourteen years old, was known in his final weeks to quote and respond to poetry more than any other thing. Meanwhile, my Uncle, John Foster, is a children's poet and my personal 'library' is full of his books that I have collected down the years.

One of my favourite subjects in high-school was English (in Scotland there is/was no distinction between Lang and Lit).

Unsurprisingly, poetry was one of the things that I most looked forward to dissecting – certainly much more than reading plays. (As an interesting side-note to this, actually, I do remember always being slightly frustrated with the interpretations of literature that we were always forced to learn. 'This is the poet's intent, and you can see this by…' But more on this below!)

It is little surprise, then, that I started writing poetry myself. I'm sure, buried somewhere in a pile of memories and photographs, there must be examples of this somewhere in the world. Unfortunately I no longer have any of my childhood scribblings. What I do have is an assortment of teenaged ramblings and angst-filled musings, most of which are epically cringe-worthy. Some of these are included here…

Poetry – both reading and writing – provides me with an outlet that I struggle to find almost anywhere else. It is part of me in a very fundamental way, and will always be with me as I move through life. The title 'Edging Gradually Towards Oblivion' reflects this – though it is being used here in a different context than in my final poem in this collection. Much like with my father, I have a sneaking suspicion that when I reach my allotted time, I will still have poems bouncing around in my head.

The Idea For This Collection

It is with all of this in mind that I started putting together the book that you now hold in your hands/on your screen. I am immensely proud of it, and what it represents for me. As my first (and hopefully not last!) collection, it includes many different poems from multiple different times in my life. As such, it shows a snapshot of the multi-layered being that inhabits my body.

When putting my thoughts together, I wanted to examine some of my experiences through the lens of poetry and explore some key aspects of being human. In the end, all of us are 'Edging Gradually Towards Oblivion' and in many ways that is a beautiful thing. We all live our lives in infinite and amazing ways, and like all good things they eventually end.

To be clear, this is not a collection about death and unhappiness. Death runs through it with reckless abandon, but so, too does Life. Even in the sadness that no doubt comes across in poems such as *Something to Get Me Through the Day* and *Trauma*, there is hope (of a sort) in the likes of *Clockwork Balloons* and *Mirror Mirror*. The angry politics of *Show Your Pride* contrasts (one way or another) with *Ode To Indifference*. Meanwhile I cannot help but to be wistful at times, as represented by *Ragnar Hates Baths*, a poem about my Bichon Frise. Finally, with *Serenity* and *Friends Are Complicated,* you will see nothing but love and joy for my wife Helen and all the people I call my friends.

As any poet will tell you, a central part of completing a collection of poetry is deciding how to present and organise the work that you want people to read. This can take a lot of different forms and structures. Some books are written chronologically, others thematically, some are before/after affairs that see-saw on a unique keystone.

This book is about my life and experiences, so you might expect it to follow a time-based structure, or else be divided by transition, politics and mental health issues.

But it isn't.

My reasoning for that is that life is chaotic. Life is messy. One moment you are laughing and having fun and the next you are crying in a shower cubicle. The same can be said of reading this collection.

Honestly, I'm not sure who I am trying to convince here: you the reader or me the writer. My intention with writing this collection, organising it, explaining it and agonising over it all ends up being but a small part of your experience of my words. You will take away your own opinions, and ultimately that is what makes poetry so wonderful.

With this in mind, I draw your attention to the 'Author's Notes' section that follows this one. As I have explained, some of these poems are highly personal to me and carry with them a very specific meaning and/or intention for me as the writer. I joked a few pages back about English teachers and trying to interpret the 'voice of the author' and I decided to include some notes on a few of my poems for this very reason.

If anyone was to look for my 'voice' then I am literally handing it to you on a plate. Not for all of them, that would be very long and very dull. Some I deliberately leave unexplained. (I see nothing wrong in leaving the odd enigma and letting you make up your own mind.) But for a select few I think some clarification may be helpful for you, the reader, to understand them better.

However, I am well aware that the subjective nature of poetry and the impact that it has on the reader is an essential part of the art form. As such I do not wish to tarnish your first experience with my words by forcing you to read them in any specific way. Thus: if you want to read these poems completely fresh and without any preconceptions, I recommend you skip the 'Author's Notes' chapter. Then come back to it at the end.

Or don't – it's entirely up to you!

Author's Notes

This is your last chance! If you are reading my work for the first time you might want to skip this! Still here? Ok, you've been warned!

Dates and Dating

The keen-eyed reader will notice that many of the poems below have dates attached to them. The even keener will notice that these are a little inconsistent. Some of this is intentional and some of it is due to the nature of my writing practices.

As my writing has developed over the years leading up to this work, I have slowly worked to develop a few good habits. One of these is writing a date next to each poem I write once I 'finish' it. This has not always been the case and as a result some of my works – even those completed recently – do not actually have a specific date attached to them. Frustration at the Me of the past is not an unfamiliar sensation (loving the double negative there!).

Yet I was left with something of a conundrum. Dates are useful, especially in a collection that contains semi-autobiographical elements such as this one. Knowing when I felt a particular emotion or drawing connections between poems written at a similar time is intriguing for me. Further, a few of my draft readers suggested to me that it enhanced their experience of the works in a few different ways. So, there we go, keep them in, sorted.

I debated not bothering with the dates at all, though. In some respects, it is messy for my poems to be presented this way. Consistency is both organisationally and aesthetically pleasing, and certainly I can see the argument for having all-or-nothing. Besides this, I asked myself, without a wider frame of reference for what was going on in my life when writing, would most readers not find the dates irrelevant and unnecessary?

My conclusion, ultimately, was to keep the dates where I had them, provide estimates for when I didn't, and leave out ones that I simply did not know.

Poems from when I was a teenager or in my early twenties are snapshots of the 'me' I was then, and decided it was important to show that. *Before the Fall* and *Nowhere to Go,* for example, both contain a huge amount of teenaged intensity, for a very good reason! When I was in my late teens and early twenties – a time when I was mostly writing 'songs' rather than 'poems' – I often focused on love and loss. Reading through many of them, and deciding which to include in this collection, I must admit it is really clear how little I knew or understood. However, that isn't a problem in some ways. Something about reading through teenaged angst is cathartic and reminds me of how far I have come – and how far I still have left to go.

Similarly, I find it cool to compare these to the poems of the 'me now'. Time is not an explicit theme of this collection, but it is there throughout and to leave out the dates completely, to me, felt like it would cheapen the ideas that are conveyed.

As I said earlier, poetry is subjective. If you like the dates, you like them. If you don't, you don't. But at least now you know my logic behind them.

Transition Towers!

It should come as no surprise that my transition features heavily in my writing. It is, after all, a huge part of my life.

For twenty-seven years I thought I was a man, then, after a period of exploration and self-discovery, I realised that I wasn't. I had pushed myself so far back into the closet during my teenaged years that I lost sight of who I was and ignored the signs that, on reflection, have always been there. I didn't have a language to describe what I felt, I had no frame of reference and even if I did I would not have had a place to figure it out.

My transition story is my own. It is different from anyone else's not because I am special but because each person's journey is distinctly unique. Yet even amongst my trans brothers and sisters, I am somewhat unusual in having only 'realised' at a relatively late age. I did not tussle with my identity as a child (that I know of) and I have not 'always known'. Mine was a gradual discovery and realisation that came after I allowed myself to explore the 'something' that I felt was wrong. I am still figuring this shit out, and I probably always will be.

Vortex, Past: Greyscale, What If..., Trauma, Hobby's Touch, What Do I Wish For? and *Empathy* were all written as part of the Trans Voices Liverpool (TVL) Project run during the Summer of 2021. This was a project ran principally by Liverpool Museums as a build up to their 2021 International Pronouns Day event. Author Marjorie H. Morgan facilitated a fantastic series of writing workshops in which I was fortunate to participate. The above named are just some of my works to come from that opportunity, all of which exploring my identity and what it means.

As with all LGBTQ issues, the politics of being transgender is fraught with challenges and this is also reflected in my writing. *Show Your Pride* and *Who Am I?* both stem from a deep frustration with all the so-called allies and the inevitable moments when they will let you down and hurt you – though usually unintentionally. Meanwhile *Secret's Out* explores the need to speak out against injustice in a world that all to readily forgets you. My anger is real and genuine, but I do have hope – some of which you can see reflected in *Mirror Mirror* (no pun intended!).

Transition is rough, bro!

I'm not mental: (I'm just a looney-tune!)

Listen, I'm not in the business of making light of mental health conditions. As much of this work shows, I know all to intimately the challenges faced by those of us for whom serotonin did a hard pass. Sometimes, though, humour is one of the best coping mechanisms on the market. When humour doesn't work – there's always poetry.

I've used it on and off as a way to cope, as a way to think through things, as a form of meditation and as a method of just getting things off my chest. As a result, as when trying to make light of it, the end result is not always reflective of the actual situation. Poetry, like any artwork, is often a constructed image – not a literal replica.

This is important to understand when reading through this collection. You can get a sense of my general feelings at the time of writing, but I warn the reader against making assumptions based on what I have written. Two of the most raw poems here are *Moving On* (written in 2009 when I was 18) and *I Remember*. Both of these might leave you worried about me and questioning a lot about my life, but both were products of the mindset I was in at the time of writing. I choose to share them here precisely for this reason.

Don't get me wrong, my brain *is* a mess. *The Mad Chameleon,* inspired by the 'Rhyme of the Ancient Mariner' by Coleridge, colourfully illustrates this point. The Mad Chameleon (sometimes simply 'The Chameleon' or 'MC') is an anthropomorphised vision of my mental health, and he is a bastard. He is always there, shifting colours and whispering in my ear. And he is damn near impossible to control. He is also fictional. I know he is not literally on my shoulder, but that doesn't mean he isn't real to me. Metalheads among my readers might recognise the idea from a lyric in a Stone Sour song – I loved it, took it and ran with it. Of course, I would be remiss not to write a poem about him.

My mental health has also been greatly affected by events in the world around me. Both in the world of work, as in

Fear Not Good Worker, and in politics, such as *The Table Saves Face* or *United We Fall, Divided We Fail.* Injustice, actual or perceived, does not sit right with me and I try to challenge it as much as possible when I see it. I am well aware that I am not perfect myself, but I try my best and do what I can.

Bakemono and *I Saw a Man Lie On a Wall*

Ekphrasis is a really interesting form of writing that uses artwork as a focal point and inspiration for a piece of poetry. I was introduced to it by a colleague (a dear friend and fellow poet) who really enjoys using strange and unique works of art to explore his themes and ideas. Not to shy away from a challenge and the prospect of something new, I decided to give it a go myself.

Bakemono

Inspiration abounds in the illustrations from Bakemono Zukushi, a painted scroll depicting yokai cryptids of Japanese folklore. Bakemono (or obake) are said to be shapeshifting creatures, of various different origins and natures and generally stalk the half-light of dusk and dawn. They are included in a cultural bank of Asian cautionary tales, or part of moralistic parables – much like La Llorona of Latin American folklore – and are a fascinating sandbox for the creative mind.

This poem focusses on Rokurokubi (ろくろくび) and Inugami (犬神) and takes the idea of old folk and 'ghost' stories and seeks to turn that on its head. It is a tale of interwoven tragedy, loss and a condemnation of how the demands of modern society stifle and destroy creativity and innovation – when they should rather nurture and empower.

I Saw a Man Lie On a Wall

Counter to this, *I Saw a Man Lie On a Wall* is much more light hearted in intention. L.S. Lowry, was a key figure in the artistic narrative of the working classes in the North West of England during the Twentieth Century. His paintings provide marvellous insights into the life and times of working men and women from this period and speak profoundly of the challenges and realities of class and industrial struggles.

Yet his paintings can also elicit a very distinct, and dare I say quite Northern –

humour. This is what I felt when I first saw 'Man Lying On a Wall' from 1957. As soon as I saw it I wondered what was going on in that man's life. I had so many questions. Why was he on a wall? Who was he? Was he supposed to be somewhere? What was going on here!? So I wrote a poem about that very response. I had great fun writing it, and for that reason it is one of my personal favourites in this collection.

A Trio Of Time

The three triolets that make up this piece are at once an experiment in this poetry form as well as a not-so-subtle play with the word 'trio'. The subject matter came to me as I was walking around the graveyard of Liverpool's Anglican Cathedral with a very dear friend of mine. Set among the gravestones and epitaphs, we came across the scene pictured below and I found myself drawn to the beautiful collision of nature, humankind and decay.

While Masonic headstones eulogised long dead 'brothers', the wooden bolsters of crumbling masonry seemed to me to be holding back the march of time itself. Yet like all things, words fade over time and names, deeds, events, families and people are all lost beneath the wear and tear of nature. In living we battle daily against the struggles and torments and all manner of difficulties, but ultimately we end up in the same place.

And that's ok.

But maybe, just maybe, we need to think about what we are leaving behind, even as we forge ahead towards our uncertain futures.

The Poems

Vortex
16.8.21

Welcome to The Vortex!
Hope you like roller-coasters
- this one is tailored for you
and you're in for quite a ride.

Think of it like an index
of neuro-chemical clusters
or hormonal fluctuation stew
draining away - like your Pride.

--> In Transition Towers
anything can happen!

A Poem of Humble and
Unparalleled Incorporeality
(aka Or Some Shit)
24.4.20

What is a poem,
But a string of words
Put together?

Some might have rhyme,
While all others need
Is metre.

But is it not
A small but meagre
Certain thing,

That, by written
Words, alone, souls
Need not sing?

OR!

Maybe I'm
Just feeling
Introspective...

MH Games
18.3.22

Abandoned…
Not deliberately.
Circumstances can't be helped,
I get that,
Hold no grudge…

Doesn't mean I don't feel.

I wanted to talk,
I geared myself up,
ready player one
of thousands, millions
across the world…

But there are no respawns
in this real-life game.

A Trio of Time

Words Live Forever

Now hear me speak, for words live forever,
Bastions 'gainst forces that seek to oppress
Emerging equalities in the human endeavour.
Now! Hear me speak, words re-sound forever,
Against the detractors whose ties we will sever,
historic imbalances that require recent redress.
Now hear me! Speak: for words live forever!
You are the bastions where they seek to oppress.

The Poets of Old

The poets of old would write in their prime,
Stretch forth vivid words, with sorrow, to preach,
A manifesto for higher ascents to climb.
The poets of old would write in their prime,
As one could they strive, fight, sing and chime,
And errors of elders could they surely impeach.
But the poets of old would, right in their prime,
Be stretched - livid words like sorrow - and preach.

The Mountains of Misbegotten Time

In youth I believed that my future was boundless
Above the mountains of misbegotten time!
I was convinced of some certain greatness.
In youth I believed. My future was. Boundless.
I'm-possible, unstoppable, opportunities countless,
I strove for the glories and triumphs sublime,
In youth. Once. I believed my future was boundless,
Entombed beneath mountains of misbegotten time.

Past: Greyscale
19.7.21

When my youth is defined,
by colours, muted and blind,
I worry that I cannot trust
my own, fractured mind.

Now I see them flourish bright,
with not a care for wrong or right,
but shining forth and seen by all
in the warmest glow of daylight.

But it took a lot to be this way,
a work in progress, day on day,
until I accept a simple truth
that I am here to stay.

My youth feels dark, shadow-cold,
First scars from merely 12 years old,
or maybe less
a potential left to mould.

The greyish blue beneath the skin,
reflects the tragic loss of kin,
while bright red oozes
beneath the blades and burns of sin.

It might be better than I think
to remember when alone I sink
from multi-coloured symmetry
into muted, blackish ink.

Can I trust my memory?
Is all this just a falsified reverie?
Or does experience fade, like aging paintings,
forever hanging, completely, heavily?

Who am I?
27.1.22

I'm just another person, really.
I was born and bred
(in Glasgow)
And one day I'll be dead and the world will
continue regardless.

So why do I matter?
What is a thought or feeling
(internal or external)
Against the backdrop of an uncaring and
unrelenting universe...

But then... why also do you matter?
If there is no absolute governing principle
(by your own logic)
then our existence in relation to each other is all but
completely irrelevant.

How does my life affect yours?
Sorry, say it again
(I missed it the first time)
I think you just admitted that it doesn't in any way:
I'm inconsequential.

Oh, wait, hold on is it a God thing?
The forgiving God who loves us all
(conveniently for you)
yet apparently rejects me and mine, also 'His'
creations, on a technicality?

So, not a God thing... what then?
I'll let you think a while
(you look like you need it)
in order for your fragile ego to seek some excuse for
denying me.

What If...
12.8.21

I wonder how it might have been
if I'd been born as I am today;
Would life be easy, calm, serene,
with all my demons held at bay?

I wonder, had I known at ten years old,
could everything have altered;
Would paths reflect the different mould,
yet nevertheless I'd faltered?

I wonder, if never I worked it out,
or despair had all consumed;
Would I have lost my final bout
and ne're the truth resumed?

Before The Fall

Whenever I think of time
I wonder how long you'll be mine.
How long will I hold you in my arms?
How long until that love does harm?

Cos you will leave me in the end
and I'll be stuck alone again.

It's amazing, the power of belief
and how it keeps us free.
So when it all comes to pass
we can be sure the memory will last.

When you are gone I will feel the burn
from a dying star who'll never learn.

But for now we are lying here –
no thoughts, no cares, no fear.
Any tears end up in the rain,
flowing, invisible, in vain.

The time will come to claim them all,
upon the ledge before the fall.

The Mad Chameleon
March 2020

The afternoon was grim, and grey,
while walking down a country road;
lost in thoughts of recent days,
my movements hunched with heavy load.

Announced beneath oppressive clouds,
That beat the mighty sun,
At last, by throwing back his shroud,
I met the Mad Chameleon.

'Hark!' said he,
'Good day my sweet,
How lovely that we now should meet
Please don't mind me, I'll take a seat,
Upon your weary shoulders.'

'And who are you,
my green-medallioned friend,
who greets me with such levity?'

'Why I am you, and now I'll lie,
Upon this spot unseen by eyes,
And ever more until we die,
I'll be your last companion.'

12

From whence he came I'll never know,
Though in some song I'd heard his name,
Perhaps by chance, by winds that blow,
He spoke to them, like me, the same.

Like some disturbed anathema, he calls,
No matter time or day,
And even Heaven's mighty halls,
His essence burns away.

And almighty Hell, with demons wrath,
would welcome him at home,
But such is not that devil's way,
Alas, he acts alone.

Day after day, he's been with me,
Night to night he's never slept,
Morning on morning, through time's wide sea,
And evermore, his promise kept.

'I know you change,'
I once observed,
'Is there a reason why?'

'It's in my nature, you bloody fool,
it's what we chameleons do!'
And with his scorn,
He changed his form,
To a violent baby blue,
With greenish flecks along his back.

His dark eyes,
Never changing,
Never moving,
Never caring.

'Alright! Alright!' I cried,
As people round me stared,
'Just back off OK, I'm sorry!'
He turned his head as if in worry,
His movements pre-prepared,
'Just fuck off! Leave me be!'

'I hate you!
Wait...
Don't go,
I need you...'

His colour changed again, at length,
To a creeping, sickly yellow,
Insipidly insidious, draining strength,
Pallid, pale and sallow.

An albatross, it once was said,
Hung round the Mariner's neck,
His painted ship, and weary head,
A hollow, lifeless wreck.

Well so it be with chameleon's tears,
That make the great bells toll,
And changing colours, through the years
 Paint, slowly, the fractious whole.

'You really won't leave, me, will you?'
'No.' He said,
Sadly,
As the yellow turned to gold.

Friends Are Complicated
10.3.22

Friendship is an amazing entity…
I have had more than a few since my beginning,
but sometimes I worry that
I seem to count them on my hands.

That statement is misleading…
Coming and going like waves on the ocean
friendship is powerful
and sometimes it is hard to differentiate;

which people fall into which categories,
which in themselves are a construction,
which makes it easier to break down
that which is impossible to quantify.

Fragmentation is resisted through persistent
contrariness
as we fight to ensure that we do not lose touch.

It is hard to say I love you…
Even more so when you are reaching
out in the dark for comfort – grasping at straws
hoping that you don't snap them;

Say it too soon at your peril...
Much like in any relationship
people can end up feeling the pressure of
three little words from another human being.

But my hands aren't big enough...
Not to envelop the pages of my love
for those around me, those who make me,
those who I don't expect to love me back.

I guess what I am trying to show is my appreciation
for people who may not spare me a second thought.

I've lost as many as I have gained...
Each occupying their own private heartbreak
- of varying sizes admittedly -
in the microcosm that comprises myself;

Do some of them even remember me..?
Actually, the fallibility of my own memory
makes it quite likely that there are those
whose faces I too have lost.

A disquieting possibility indeed...
By forgetting someone's face
might that mean that, somehow,
you have forsaken part of their souls?

Weirder still are those friends who I feel like I have
but they don't even know I exist.

Such is the bizarrity of social media...
Folks from across the globe see and are seen,
never to meet in person
yet quite genuinely their lives entwine;

Shared content, experiences, likes, interests,
loves...
All that might unite two people in a room
now emerge through corporate screens
creating tipping surface pressure that never stops;

Though I'm not complaining, I can't help but
wonder...
How amazing is the world now that face to face,
previously the bare minimum for human connection
is seemingly a thing of the past.

Perhaps what I'm expressing doesn't make sense…
(I'm not the first to say that friends are
complicated.)

Trauma
13.8.21

Trauma comes in many forms.
Did you know that?
I didn't...
Worlds torn apart do not
always have to be huge.
They can be but a wing-beat
on a broken drum,
or a patter of August rain
against the backdrop
of historic, sometimes histrionic
blackouts, long forgotten
beneath the sands.

Moving On
2009

I don't know how I feel,
but my life just seems too real,
and nothing I can do can satisfy my guilt.

I know that I love her,
but emotion only hurts,
so I'm learning to hide it all
away from their thoughts.

Because if I show them my pain
it just hurts all the more,
and if I tell them the truth
then I'll crumble;
If I'm honest with myself
I know it's much too late -
I hope that my death comes soon...

I think I've lived too long,
and I know I've done things wrong,
I've broken too many things that I just can't repair.

I've lost the one I need,
the only voice I'd heed,
If I ever really had it
from the start anyway.

So there's nobody else
I can talk to anymore,
and there's nobody else
who can save me;
If I'm honest with myself
I've been alone all along -
I hope that my death comes soon…

I am sorry to everyone,
I would give it one last run,
 but I feel so alone in my heart and my soul.

All of them will stare,
but none will really care,
about the hole that's been growing
since I drew my first breath.

The first mistake I made
was the be all alone;
the second was to think
that you could fix me.
But if I'm honest with myself
I know I'm not worth the time -
so I hope that my death comes soon…

The walls have broken down.
Now I'm leaving town.
I'll go alone, I don't need you to come with me.

I'm tired of all of this,
I've never felt any bliss,
like all the stupid people tell me
that I should know by now.

So it's time for me to fly away
and find my new home;
It's time for me to bid you all
farewell.
And if I'm honest with myself
I should have done this long ago -
so I hope that my death comes soon.

Bakemono
August 2021

Huddled forms in a mighty place,
Where tales are told of beasts galore,
Two companions for nightmares race,
Forever searching, wanting more.

When bathing in the starry rays,
Warm and solar, redeeming gold,
Piece by piece and phase by cruel phase
Their spirits morph to crystal, cold.

They shift midst restless reverie,
Despoiling all that is sacred,
Choking on careless revelry,
Seething with a boundless hatred.

The suehirogari-screams alone,
Are enough to strangle the dead,
Inspiring the path to sins atone,
 Spinning the yarns of folklore's thread.

Beautiful, elegant and true,
Ineffable beyond her years,
Warrior stock built through and through,
The finest mind among her peers.

She gazed upon the shadowed form,
Her façade sallow and sickly,
Its billowed coat that's never warm,
Slowly oozing, bleeding, thickly.

Together had they lived as one,
Sheltered in eternal wonder,
Till growth of fouler hearts were done,
Sky-high rent them asunder.

Pathetic jealous petty greed,
Re-birthed inside the seed of man,
Alas an unpaid mouth to feed,
Was 'too much' for his paltry clan.

Sharpened, a mithril fire shimmered,
A cursing blow that life defeats,
Woeful final dreams delivered,
As blood spilled out across the sheets,

Guardian, hero, protector,
But helpless to prevent her plight,
Locked away, a banished spectre,
Subsisting in the half-moon light.

Exploding forth, a mournful howl,
From deep within the cord of life,
Shapeless, fading, and run afoul,
Of fortune's fickle blazoned knife.

But neither one did end that day,
Though not for the wont of trying,
In mirthless depths of myth they lay,
Condemned, alone, undying.

So listen close to long-lost tales,
Gird against the follies of youth,
Remember well the hollow wails,
Of those beholden without truth.

And if at night your mind does stray,
Upon paths you find untrodden,
Take care, for welcome cannot stay,
 Towards those whose cores are rotten.

Brindled Fury
2.6.21

Shaking, she stalks the hallways:
Brindled Fury.
Jaundiced, bubbling
Not even beneath the surface
Un-stable and seething.
Trying not to keep composure
Trying not to keep explo…

Sure;
So sure of righteous entitlement
Sure that someone else bears the blame
(Actually they do…)
Sure to wear her best face forward,
Sure to put her happy frown upside-down;
Trying not to keep losing grip
of the only thing she values --- sure!

Every mistake is logged and noted,
Trimmed and trotted –
An allusionary illusion of false control.
Brindled Fury blazes,
A super-novic shot of novocaine
Direct to the jugular.
No vocative hero stands a chance

As she burns to ashes
The very bridges that she stands upon.

Crying, she holds her head in painful pose,
Erratic movement,
Must hurt to be so suddenly unveiled
A lightning flash;
Unbridled:
Fragility – that her fragile mind won't let her see –

Mottled, sallow, shallow, sickly.
Unhealthy as the world to which she screams,
A toxic sludge of slurried slurrs
Character Assassination
Bystanders, innocent collateral damage –
Or witnesses to the crime.

Yet unclear the very same is undefined,
Rattles deathly – furious chimes
of a brindled clock-face – can't unwind,
Can't rewind,
Can't pre-wind,
Unravelling beneath the weight of time;
Which never grants itself enough.

Unimaginably profound pity flows;
There is no hate, there is no anger,
(Not direct or targeted)
No fury…
But merely understanding that fact -
She doesn't have a choice.
She doesn't know her actions.
She doesn't have a voice.
She DOES have a chance –
but not the wherewithal to take it.

Exhaustion weeps, then, from every ounce,
Energy expended beneath the heavy lids.

I am sorry I cannot help you more.
But there is nothing more that I can…
Help.

Vilanelle To My Current Mood
24.5.21

At times I'm found wanting, and shit out of luck,
With nothing of substance to say,
But, you must understand, I just don't give a fuck.

I'm searching for something, the right phrase to pluck,
The words I've been chasing all day,
Yet for rhymes I'm still wanting, I'm shit out of luck.

There no sense in waiting, no deals to be struck,
I might as well give up and pray!
Bugger it all for now: I just don't give a fuck.

In the back of my mind like secrets I tuck,
Some ideas that are anxious to play,
But alas they're left wanting, they're shit out of luck.

You know what, I'm tired, be gone spiteful Puck,
Go find the some other affray,
And give no excuses I just don't give a fuck.

So if in your metre you're perfectly stuck,
Unable to make your own way,
Then maybe you're wanting, and shit out of luck,
But you must understand: I just don't give a fuck!

Hobby's Touch
23.7.21

Hobbies are a funny thing –
    They Excite
    They Drive
    They Emote
    They Express.

Here I am now – writing
       - though I wish to do more…-
as part of my many activities.

Hobbies are important to us –
    They are Tactile
    They are Physical
    They are Real
    They are Grounding
    They are Rounding.

Sitting beneath a standard lamp
      - fond memories of painting
        models -
I haven't done that since coming out…

Hobbies give us meaning and purpose –
     They Anticipate
     They Extrapolate
     They Motivate
     They Elaborate
     They Obfuscate.

Is it possible to feel another's soul?
               - Through a terrarium of
                    moss balls? -
Of course: creativity is in the beholder and
                    creator.

Hobbies do not lie, as a rule –
     They Reveal
     They Revel
     They Explore
     They Entertain
     They Enlighten.

People are brought together so meaningfully
               - disparate, different
                    or direct -
Magnificently demonstrating… You aren't
                    alone!

Self-Care
18.3.22

Self-care comes back tomorrow;
tonight, I drink my wine.

> I try in vain to drown my sorrow
> or seek some peace divine.

My wings get broken in the storm:
they never truly healed before.

> I drift and flutter, lost, forlorn
> to rest at last upon the floor.

I know that I can ride this out:
a path well-trod for me to follow.

> So please, don't worry, no need to shout
> for self-care, at last, comes back

tomorrow.

Blues and Coffee
20.3.22

There is something inherently satisfying
about a strong coffee and loud blues
in an Irish Bar in Liverpool on a Sunday.
It's speaks to me in profound ways,
a link to the past that I never had,
the lie of false nostalgia.

When I was younger these times
sometimes led to heavy booze,
self-destructive tenancies
that led to a metaphorical gutter
the likes of which a middle-class
University student knows nothing about.

I used to know a woman who sang the blues,
she used to joke that all she needed
was a strong drink
and a man to knock her around -
I think she managed to find both once.

I sip my coffee, Aretha Franklin blasting
through the speakers during a refresh
R.E.S.P.E.C.T
The double-bassist tells me to smile,
which annoyingly works
despite the low-brand sexism.
(I might be being a bit harsh there actually...)

Meanwhile I am dying for a cigarette,
even though I've never been a smoker.
A controlled and controllable vice
that I can oversee, I can choose,
long term those things'll kill you,
but the odd one can't hurt, can it?

I wonder where that woman is now...
We lost touch a long time ago,
with no way to really reconnect.
I wonder if this is what it is like to get old...

One day I might find out,
but for now I just need to get out of my head,
blues by definition is transitory,
moving from place to place without anchor
or somewhere to call home.
Meanwhile I, thankfully, have both.

Aesthetic
12.2.22

An aesthetic can change multiple times,
but that doesn't make it invalid.

Many different manifestations of personality
can be reflected in various aspects
of ever shifting amalgams of different genres.

Whether it be music, fiction, history, whatever
experiences are real!

They make up what people make of them
- the emotional connection to something
matters completely and truly,
sometimes more honestly than
many of our routine responses.

It might only be fleeting -
days, months or minutes within a lifetime;
hundreds of thousands of possibilities
all of them awesome!

Many of us have been the weirdos,
the ones outside the norm,
the ones who don't conform,
the ones who take the time

to figure out what we want
and make mistakes or change our minds.

Or sometimes, quite simply,
we find our solace in something new.

So please please
please explore,
find your niche,
and if it isn't for you,
or you get lost in something else,
move on
without fear.

Mozart 2133
26.4.21

They work non-stop,
Pounding to the ones and zeros,
Exquisite and mathematical
Melancholy,
Smooth as arias constructed long ago,
Bludgeoning the senses
In peaceful harmony,
Transmitted over seconds
To anyone who'll listen.

Burnout
30.11.21

I'm sitting, gingerly in a field of glass,
glinting with the winter sun and bitter wind.

I'm lying, fearfully, on a bed of needles,
constructed just for me, by me, in me.

I'm running, fitfully, on a molten treadmill,
forever tipped on the edge of burning cacophony.

I'm swimming, drowning in an ocean of known
unknowns
that freezes urgently with each inevitable wave.

I'm dying just as much as I am living,
within a cage of pestilent virtue.

I'm standing. I'm standing. I'm standing.
Despite the better judgement urging me to fall.

I'm watching for the smallest shimmer
of distant recognition or understanding.

Mirror Mirror
July 2021

Tales are told of Alice
and her looking-glass of wonder,
but with these words I apologise,
I've come to steal her thunder.

It's been a long time coming,
though longer than I know,
'twas only about three years ago,
that thoughts began to grow.

I used to think me ugly,
abhorrent and obscene,
But now I feel quite pretty
(if humbly) and serene.

Looking in the mirror,
there is quite the sight to see,
A young(ish) emerging woman,
staring back at me.

Of Kilts and Skirts
16.8.21

A kilt is not a skirt,
or so I used to insist.
Now I always wear skirts
(or dresses)
with a kilt being up there
on my sartorial wish list.
A kilt is not a skirt, I said,
and a blouse is not a shirt!

Brooke's First Day At Work
February 2022

Brooke was a brand-new member of staff
who came in for his very first day,
and though he was cute and treated with love,
at first on a desk he decided to stay!

For being a badger, nocturnal at heart,
he spent his first shift fast asleep;
but when night came around, his energy found
in the Priory museum he began to creep.

With candle in paws – beeswax and handmade –
he snuffled about in a search
for a perfect new spot that he could call home
and then watch all the guests from his perch.

He peeped out from a vase, but it was too high,
on display cases he had no grip,
tile oven's too hot, and the statue's too big
building arches was hurting his hip!

He slunk back to the office to rethink his plan,
though truly he'd had so much fun,
so he'll keep up the search, let you know how it goes
until finally the best spot is won!

Ragnar Hates Baths
12.4.22

His tail droops when he realises;
which takes some time
for a cottonwool bud
with pretentions of sentience.

His eyes seem to shimmer with sadness;
though of course
this is simply projection
of anthropomorphisation.

His brow furrows as he's filled with dismay:
some times it is hard to tell,
his soft fur is so floofy
it is little more than a twitch.

His paws seem to turn to lead:
you could almost be forgiven
for thinking this literally
when they are really mucky.

His body becomes a dead weight:
as he is led (or dragged)
up the stairs towards
inevitable doom.

You see, to him this is pure torture:
 a waterboarding abuse
of his imagined autonomy
and fluffy rights.

Problem is, he's a smelly, grubby boi:
so hate it as he does,
sometimes he just needs
a fucking bath!

The Table Saves Face
31.8.21

The world is not made for the people like me,
The people who call out the things that they see,
The sight of which breaks down the will just to be, The
being of something as vocal as we.

And so must we sit with our frail malcontent,
Do what we must, nevermind our consent,
Sacrifice all for a system that's bent,
Slave as we cry till our life-blood is spent.

So in our own minds we begin an affray,
As if that will keep us till end of the day,
But then we are punished with games that you play, in
facets accepted if wanting to stay.

The choices are few, if there's any at all,
The choices are made when you don't heed the call,
Yet choices are wasted when met with a wall,
Choices mean nothing 'neath mountains too tall.

So say I again that the world has no place,
For all those who struggle to keep up the pace,
For all of our effort just ends with disgrace,
While our scraps are tainted; the table saves face.

I Walk The Line – Aisla's Version
21.3.22

(To be read/sung with Johnny Cash's classic song
firmly in mind, and re-worked with the utmost
respect and love for the original!)

I keep a close watch on this gender of mine,
I keep my eyes fixed upon it all the time,
I keep the world outside so I can shine,
Because it's mine, I walk the line.

I find it really quite a challenge to feel true,
I find support that all seems too see-through
Yes, I'll admit it's exhausting to teach you,
Because it's mine, I walk the line

As sure as night is dark and day is light
I tread on eggshells round you day and night
Because experience I've known just proves it's right
Because it's mine, I walk the line.

I've got a way to keep you on my side,
I try to make you love what I can't hide
For if I don't, I know that you might turn the tide,
Because it's mine, I walk the line.

I keep a close watch on this gender of mine,
It keeps being questioned by folks all the time,
I keep my hopes up so one day I'll be fine,
Because it's mine, I walk the line.

Ode to Indifference
21.2.22

I hate to be the one to tell you this,
I would love for it not to be,
but the only emotion I feel right now
is indifference twixt me and thee.

There's little point in mincing words,
but even less in standing ground,
since of the fucks I have to give
not one for you is found.

The turd is huge, that weighs heavy on me
and it takes a while to flush,
yet down it goes, without my help,
I see no need to rush.

I could say more to make my point,
and use my wicked wordy art,
but frankly that's just too much effort,
so I'll just leave you when I part.

Crashing
14.3.22

Crashing:
- feels like -
- a tonne of bricks -
- has been clipped -
- onto my brain -

Crashing:
- feels like -
- a snail had possessed me -
- sluggishly and slowly -
- as thoughts grind
down the gears -

Crashing:
- feels like -
- every joint is seizing -
- every muscle cramping -
- every heartbeat
a tolling bell -

Crashing:
- feels like -
- only hours ago
the world was mine -
- now I am its hostage -
- and it wants
revenge -

Crashing:
    - feels like -
        - just being dramatic -
            - nothing is wrong -
                - you are lying for
                      attention -

Crashing:
    - feels like -
        - why are you crying -
            - pull yourself together -
                - you are just so
                    very immature –

Crashing:
    - feels like -
        - help -
            - help me -
                - please, someone
                    anyone

                          Help.

                          Me.

Do Unto Others…
3.3.22

Is this how you would treat your daughter:
Discard her like a used scrap of toilet roll
without a care or a thought for the consequences,
Grind her down for weeks,
holding your power over her
knowing that she is worthless to you,
belittling and downplaying,
setting her up to fail,
making her hate you so much that once the axe
drops
she is almost glad to lose her head
rather than spend another moment in your
company?

Well, she's 18 now, it's not your responsibility,
you don't have to be compassionate
nor must you show basic human decency;

She's always known that the day will come
when you pack her bags for her
and show her the door,
so really she should have seen this coming;

Obviously it is her fault, not yours and there was
nothing you could have done to make it better.

And what about the effect on her sister:
is that too much for you to bother considering,
as she's already leaving,
she's seen you for what you are
and flees the nest as fast as humanly possible
all so that she doesn't have to bathe in your toxicity
any longer than she absolutely has to
for legal compliance?

No, of course not
– because she is immaterial to your goals:
Little Miss Trouble who fails to stand by
and put up with your ridicule and incessant
demands.
You learned not to touch her,
knowing full well
that she won't hesitate to bite back,
and call you out on all your bullshit.

Do unto others as you would have done to you.
Karma's a bitch,
and sooner or later your house of cards
is going to crumble -
or better yet, underneath the tides of change
will sink, soggy and malformed,
into the shingle-sands of memory.

It's Cold On The Streets In Winter
30.11.21

It's cold on the streets in winter.

It's cold on the streets at any time of year.
I sit with myself a moment and thank my luck,
- for all the things that I have
- and those that I didn't
and those that I pray
(to a god that I don't believe in)
that I will never face.

Because it's cold on the streets in winter.

To Brief Reprieve
Summer 2020

Shall we sing tales of how the hours were spent,
Alone with nought to keep us safe, but fears?
For Summer's wonder must we now repent,
and curse the days we had to dry the tears?

It seems we took the chance to throw the towel,
A gauntlet versus viral's killing spree;
Beneath the sun we bathed to wash afoul,
To rinse the eyes of horrors all could see.

So thus we smiled, we read, we talked, we wrote –
uncarved, the distance holding fast like stone;
Our souls combined as one by one we note
an end to cares for which we now atone.

In naïve hope, we dreamed the battle won;
Believing not that death had just begun.

Unnecessary Evil
8.6.21

In a time of fractured boundaries,
Resolute in the sweeping, inevitable onslaught,
Of unseen extermination,
Denied until a Colossus, unspoken
Breached its waves upon ignorant shore,
And taking taking taking,
I found myself becoming, emerging,
Reshaped as I need to be.

As one we volunteered our rights,
For the greater good, that still remains
Within us all, surrounding
Spreading with intent to stop us growing,
A fight that no one wins, no one can,
Only loss and loss and loss
That tries to sound the closing bell
Of the humanitarian experiment.

Imploding, collapsing, disintegrating,
Everything stood stock still,
And all that was left was the wait,
Stretched thin already but pulling tighter,
Delayed and held back for want of ignorance,
Falling further and further and further,

Into the abyssal oblivion
that lies behind false glories.

Yet from the ashes emerges a truth,
Universal and self-evident, of sorts,
Eternal in the making of the one,
Reflecting in the desires of the many,
And unyielding in the obvious requirement,
Validation, reality, validation, reality,
Simple words on a page that express
The very fundamental value of a soul.

I am here to stay, expanding my universe,
Extending my reach to those who must hear it,
A fragile voice, booming in the deep,
Laced with a vaccine against the world.
They cannot erase me, much as they try,
I shout, I shout, I shout,
My own body is changing as it must,
Alone, but united in solidarity.

Observation Cynicism
2009

(Inspired by Bob Dylan's 'It's Alright Ma (I'm
Only Bleeding)'

Words don't mean anything anymore,
but I still write here and try to implore,
while lyrics serve merely to restore
a gentle wall against all that we abhor,
a break from thought of those who die at war
and the heathens who command them.

While I steal words from others' lines,
indoctrination paints your minds,
persuading there's no need to look behind,
while sunlight seems no more to shine
behind clouds of smoke, rhetoric and rhyme
that we are all forced to contend with.

But I refuse, yes I refuse,
to give myself in to all your truths,
and I will shout, yes I will shout,
as lies and talk build walls to keep us out.

The words scribbled on the pages scream,
while death camps show the fitful dream
and corporations wipe the dirty screen
to muddy further the crusting sheen
as diseases in those forests teem
and the innocent are left on killing-floors dying.

And all this needs to be said again,
while people all put paper to pen
only to be thrown out alone to fend
against useless, bureaucratic lies in ten-
fold promises of evil men
who laugh at us for even caring.

But I deny, yes I deny,
those men to have a right to cry;
for they must see, yes they must see
the bleak and day-to-day reality.

Our sovereignty rose as lights were dipped
in false stories, analysed and stripped
of validity to all who live in the crypt
of knowledge fabricated, timed and clipped
to pinboard pockets still to be ripped
in full view of your temples.

While God stands by, leaving all to drift,
on splintered pages of worn-out script
that say we'll die for simply daring to exist
from shattering waves that batter minds with swift,
forceful, tense judgment, while liberty sifts
through all your malevolent intentions.

And I proclaim, yes I proclaim,
that I can't be alone with my disdain,
yet still I doubt, and yet I doubt,
that there'll be anyone left to shout.

Poem For Ukraine
25.2.22

A tribute to the brave men and women of a beautiful
country.

The Breadbasket is burning…
It wasn't built to withstand tanks
and guns
and missiles;
A rich and fruitful history
is woven into its very fabric -
a noble people reaped
like the harvests they sowed.

Lies, layer upon layer upon layer…
a reverse-styled nesting doll
where
every layer is bigger
every layer is thicker,
every layer more brazen,
every layer more deadly.

The Breadbasket is burning,
Yet passivity fans the flames…

We stand together and stand united…
but we are not the ones torn asunder -
torn by plunder,
all to satisfy the whims of a greedy despot
that clings to days long passed -
like some demented, power-hungry relic
of a bygone age.

The Breadbasket is burning,
while the high and mighty play games…

Our very own are tainted with the stink…
Its hard to hold the high ground
when you're sinking in the mire,
paddling harder and harder
against and endless current
 that always seems to run
downhill
befouling the very gutter that you try to call home.

The Breadbasket is burning,
but the match too far to snuff...

The Breadbasket is burning,
when will enough,
finally,
truly,
at last,
ever,
be enough?

If...
(A Millennial Prayer)
June 2009

If we are the future
then the past is doomed;
If they are the past
then our present is ruined;
If you are the present
then God help us all;
we're sitting here waiting
for a mighty big fall.

If this is the time
then where does it go?
If this is the place
then you must let me know;
If you are the way
to set us all free,
then why won't you come here
and die alongside me?

Ah – You're too busy to come to the phone.
Let me guess – You don't really want to know.
We have all these words
that we have to tell,
that rebound forever
on your impenetrable shell.

If weaker men have guns,
that you personally have sold;
If young men are dying
as well as the old;
If poor men are fighting,
for the right just to live;
then how can you ever
expect us to forgive?

If you keep your job
while the people are starving;
If we're all left wondering
while bells ring, alarming;
If lies born and bred
from your pockets are spawned
then how else do you think
we're going to respond?

Yes – If the same were to happen to you;
Really? – You'd use us to silence the coup.
Those very same people
you claim to protect,
are lining the streets
that you seem to reject.

If you could step aside
to let a newer flame burn;
If you could just leave,
accept you've had your turn;
but if you can do nothing
to amend your course -
then why can't we change it
by will or by force?

If I'm getting tired
of this old routine;
If I'm looking forward
to the end of your regime;
If I see a truth
that just needs to be told -
then can you accept
that your vision is old?

Alas – The damage has already been done.
You! – You've pulled at the trigger of that loaded
gun!
It's too late for us
we'll just have to pray;
for the next generation
to salvage the day.

Serenity
11.3.22

You are my Serenity,
as we journey
through the galaxy;

My rock, my anchor,
my guiding North Star,
you keep me grounded.

Like a wayward sailor,
the beacon of your love
will always bring me hope;

Even on the darkest night
beset by storms,
I will find you.

You are my Serenity,
and the universe
it knows;

For you discovered me –
my love,
and every day it grows.

Secrets Out

I've felt muzzled, on and off,
Like a wounded dog, punched to the edge
Lashing out in desperate self-defence and sadness,
But yet just another statistic,
And every innocence analysed and ripped apart,
Devoid of context and twisted beyond recognition,
In pursuit of a scapegoat that stifles progress.

Freedom of speech is never free,
If you are at the bottom of the food chain,
Whether by design, or circumstance
Or just bad luck.

Old stereotypes and ignorant sidelines
Re-emerge for a new audience, a fresh glut of hate
It will not die with the growing list of names
That get lost in the media indifference,
While this little light flickers in the void
And treads the eternal, existential trapeze
Urgent, the vital requirement of living.

Underneath (or above?) my little universe,
Systemic denial of a lived experience
Becomes tid-bit scraps of justice that can't get over
'I can't breathe'.

Mine is my own, a source of pride and joy,
Choosing to become myself, metamorphose,
Close doors of past pain, without hiding,
And, while incognito, discovered
As all good truths will 'out' – but only in obscurity,
I do the right thing and cover the bases,
A luxury privilege and I cling for dear life.

Some stories need to be told, though,
Whether by explicit words under a bended knee,
A rainbow standard on a bright summer day,
Or through silence.

Nowhere To Go
2010

I've been sitting for a long time,
wondering what's going on.
And I've been asking myself
who is right and what is wrong.

While no answers seem to come.
nothing I see seems to show
where we were standing
and what I failed to know.

I'm lost in this mystery
and trapped in the depths of this hole.
I'm burning inside,
but there's no-place to hide
and I've nowhere to go.

I've been waiting for far too long
for someone to show us the way.
And I've been wishing, as the tears fall,
it was over yesterday.

But there's no hope for me now;
I've got no place in this world.
I'm weary of your pain,
and your body all beaten and curled.

You're lost in this mystery.
You're trapped in the very same hole.
You're burning inside,
but there's no-place to hide
and you've nowhere to go.

I've been seeing almost every day
some new brand of failure.
I've been wondering about what we must have missed
in the moments we felt so tender.

When we brought them forward
we knew how it was going to be;
'till finally, when we were older,
our eyes were too blistered to see –

That we're lost in this mystery.
We're trapped in the deepening hole.
We're burning inside,
but there's no-place to hide
and you've nowhere to go.

So I'm hoping, for this child's sake,
that the world still turns around.
I'm praying, for this world's sake,
we'll be six feet in the ground.

'Cos we've caused all this mess
that we are not destined to clean,
and one day in that future
our legacy will no-longer be seen.

We'll be lost in this mystery.
We'll be buried in our very-own hole.
We'll be burning inside,
while there's no-place to hide
and there's nowhere to go.

God In The Machine
28.4.21

The poetry of image
Boggles the mind.
With
Without
With-ever-more.
Narrative-sounding dissonance
And 'Industrial Prose.'
Pumped out of insignificant
Insignificance
To meet the maker-creator-victim.

Fear Not Good Worker
9.9.21

Fear not, good worker, your world is fine,
especially when you're kept in line;
the gas is only for troublers lit –
those who dare to call out the bullshit;
while naked, sitting alone with hubris enthroned,
your wicked ways come ne're condoned
you're in the wrong – you dared to speak
and words alone are frail and weak,
so take the beatings doled out with pride,
you're lucky: they get it worse on the other side.

Bowling
19.3.22

Last night, I bowled
a perfect strike!

Wanna know how?

I shouted 'fuck you'
at the top of my lungs

imagining the pins
were my enemies' heads.

Then I went back to normal.

I am terrible at bowling!

I Am Going to Miss You All
21.3.22

My time has been served
and duty is done,
I've learned a lot,
I've lost and I've won;

The last day has come
and my heart is a-glow,
I will miss you all dearly,
but now I must go,

I've had my challenges,
too many to name,
I've played the age-old
strategic game;

I've taken on more
than I can chew,
I've sat at times
with nothing to do;

I've screamed the Earth
and cursed the moon,
I've turned it around
in one afternoon;

I've laughed and cried
then laughed again,
I've seen some starlet-students
wax and wain;

I've started out
with blondie whisps,
I've grown it out,
now dark and crisp;

I've put on weight
and lost some more,
I've sorted through data
- what a bloody bore;

I've used my skills
to teach the class,
I've waited for students
sitting on my arse;

I've joined the union,
been the EDI rep,
I've dodged poop and glass
with every step;

But more than this,
so much more than it all
there is one thing about leaving
that'll sure make me bawl;

I met in my colleagues
the true cream of the crop,
a handful of people
who come out on top,

I'll see you all soon,
though for now we must part,
So thank you, my friends,
from the bottom of my heart.

I Saw A Man Lie On A Wall
24.6.21

Inspired by L.S. Lowry: 'Man Lying on a Wall,
1957'

I saw a man lie on a wall,
he must have been but five feet tall.
Had he no cares if he should fall?
Alas seemed not, no none at all!

Although the sky was grey with rain,
the umbrella was propped without a stain,
while any thoughts (damp, cold or pain?)
like pesky bugs he did disdain.

Emblazoned on his smart beige case
an L.S.L. in black did grace,
the rest was left as empty space,
save scuffmarks on the out-worn base.

Unto the sky, there rose some smoke,
a pillar, halted with every toke,
like matchstick men each drawn bespoke,
  from fags that from his mouth did poke.

I wondered if his brain was fried,
Through stress or sorrow deep inside.
Or if, indeed, he'd simply died,
but kept on moving, just from pride.

Probably not, his diaphragm moved his hat,
which made him look so oddly fat,
but at least it could be discerned that
we didn't need an ambulance, stat!

Who was this man, I hear you ask,
that lay upon a wall to bask?
Well now it is my life-long task,
his means and motives to unmask.

No-one asked wherein he worked!
Perhaps in some studio factory he lurked,
all his important duties blithely shirked!
It's no bloody wonder he smirked!

(Meanwhile, the ticking clock of time,
suggested noon has passed it's prime.
I doubt he earned a single dime,
if his bosses learned of his crime!)

Of where he lived, it can't be far,
from where industrial landscapes are!
Oh, and isn't it quite bizarre:
He's a shoddy knock-off Ringo Starr!

Forgive me, please, for your time taken,
His countenance had left me shaken.
I never checked if he will waken,
lest all my efforts be forsaken!

What do I Wish For?
10.8.21

A world more human
but also less 'man';
A truth universal
but also of Earth;
A chance to be hopeful,
with more for the hopeless;
A right to keep living
without liberty dying;
I want to understand you.
I want you to understand me.

Empathy
9.8.21

Why do you hate me?
Genuinely, I want to know.
Is your bile complete consumption
or is there hope for you still?

Can you try to understand me?
Here, let me help.
See? We're not so different, you and I.
Yet here we stand – opposites on invisible
lies.

Inspiring Revulsion
30.11.21

Some emotions repulse me;
their fervour boils my blood
Yet accompany cold, freezing, icy
dread.

In the blizzard I stand alone;
there are things and thoughts
that you can't speak aloud -
festering.

Rot, a very real experience,
laces unbeknownst compulsion
of fleeting words that inspire
revulsion.

I would not put them to page;
I would not even if I could,
for fear of what I know would be
condemned.

Righteously, purposefully, justly;
the abhorrent visage reflects
a deeper, darker, desire -
vilification.

Forgive me please, you untold will;
for feeling doesn't lead to acts,
but sits, in calm disquiet, beneath
re-evaluation.

Rest In Power
In Memoriam of Imogen Christie d. July 2021
2.8.21

Rest In Power,
my would-be friend.
Your mantle remains
resplendent and eternal.

I did not know you well.
To be honest,
I did not really know you
at all.

Profoundly, this makes me sad.
We met only a few times,
through computer screens,
but your name resounded.

Resounded.
Like a piper's call
thro' English glen
affecting change.

Yet I believe still that we'll meet one day;
In mind or in spirit
in a world forever improved
by your – by our – continued fight.

Show Your Pride
14.12.21

Raise a flag and show your pride,
give thanks to all who grant you leave;
yet in their secret hearts deride,
with wicked smiles, what you believe.

Raise your toast to your good friends,
who say the words and light the flame;
denying petty odds and ends
to beat you down for their own fame.

Raise your head, so calm and strong,
become exactly what they want to see;
Then one small slip betrays the throng,
Of hoards who tell you 'you are free'.

They clap you, firmly, from behind,
in irons you yourself have rung,
For God forbid it slips your mind
to hold your calloused, bloody tongue.

United We Fall, Divided We Fail
January 2022

(My first poem written in Scots)

Ah'm a Scot, but no enough a Scot,
for in England dae ah dwell,
an for mah sins, wae Diels the lot,
som damn me aw tae Hell.

Mah blud rins red wae flecks o' gold,
but neither rins thegither;
yet in their savage rivals old
all hearts bleed oot foriver.

Union's but a dirty word
to hide an unco bitter truth:
whar mair demanded splits the world
mair fractured a' mah dreams o' youth.

Even though I feel the bite
o' division that snaps the haun that feeds it,
a dowie voice suggests it might
be the only way for thems as needs it.

United we fa', divided we fail
an truces both sides aw' rebute
the battle's set in ships tae sail
on mindfu' fields the fighters put,

the pickets a' be doon the line,
lang laid 'fore plans o' mice and men,
the young get auld and dae just fine
so cycles a' repeat again.

We've faught and died and faught oor ain,
Cullodden, Somme and Middle East
till hiltie-skiltie through the rain
we find oorsels afore the Beast

that hauds a mirror up tae oor face,
the horrors of oor mind tae steer,
tae flewit; far-off vain disgrace
in a' the 'liberty' that we haud dear.

Ah didnae want tae be this way -
a better world's within oor grasp!
But petty problems, day on day,
just sting us like the damnit wasp!

So listen gud mah war'ly frien,
and listen while ah tell ye straight;
A world united we nivir hae seen,
but division's no oor only fate!

I Remember
'Finished' August 2021

I remember the day that I almost killed myself.
Not the whole day,
not even what happened to start it,
but I remember the moment.
I remember getting a camera-bag strap,
checking it was strong,
making a loop and hanging it
from the banister of the stairwell
and looking at it,
like it was the last line of hope in my sinking world.
I remember choosing not to kill myself that day.
Not because I was brave,
nor because I found some particular reason
to stay alive
as such,
but because I was afraid.
Afraid of the pain,
afraid of what would happen,
afraid that I would be found.
I remember crying and wanting to escape.

I remember years earlier when I first cut myself.
It wasn't really out of specific anger
or sadness
or hatred.

I don't know why I did it, in fact.
It was just one of those things
that I did.
I remember taking a broken protractor
 and pulling it against the skin
on the back of my hand
and then being stopped by school-friends.
People asked me why,
interrogated me,
told me never to do it again.
I remember doing it again.
I don't know when the 'first' time was.
I don't know if it was spontaneous,
if I was inspired to do it
by someone or something.
But I know that I did.
And it became a habit.
It was something that I would do
to soothe myself,
to expel the burning that I felt in my head and my heart.
But I was never very 'good' at it.

I remember the age of 17
until I was around 19.
I drank a lot.

When I stayed in a disabled persons' home
in Germany,
with beer that I could legally buy
(and my self-taught guitar skills);
my main escape from
crushing loneliness of being
in a foreign country,
for the most part away from anyone
my own age,
and with next to nothing to do.
I remember drinking because,
like the old cliché states,
it helped me to forget.
To forget what a shit person I was –
how much I hated myself –
the life that I was living.
But also to forget
I had a shield in front of me at all times,
that hid what was really going on,
a shield that came crashing
down
in fits of depression,
tears and anger
driving people away from me.

I remember sneaking to the doctor
in order to get medical help
for my depression.
I remember being told
I was just
'struggling to get over'
the loss of my father.
Wounded though I was,
limping day by bloody day
across a void
that grown adults struggle to navigate,
I remember being dismissed,
ignored
and left to my own self-care
with no equipment with which
to execute it.
I was worried that my diagnosis would
cause anger;
so I never got diagnosed,
despite heavy medication
and never sought out real help.
Gradually I learned to accept
the unacceptable,
embracing my broken mind
as a fundamental part of myself,
resolving
to use it for the greater good –

wasting my time
trying to fix the world
when I can't even fix myself.

Hey You...
23.8.21

I'm not sure what to tell you.
I'm not sure *how* to tell you.
There's a lot that's changed,
a lot that's different,
and so much that stays the same.

People come and people go.
You come and you go.
Like a fire, blazing a trail
through your own story,
unpredictable and uncontrolled.

Things tend to work out.
But not always as they are supposed to.
Remember, there is still time,
as the seasons pass year on year,
it's never too late to fly.

You'll feel tied down.
You'll feel untethered.
The brick wall will meet
the endless mountain trail
in a cacophony of choices.

Strength abounds in ways unimagined.
Weakness remains to break the fall.
A yin-yang honesty is contrast
to the untold lies and hidden facts
that happen one way or another.

Clockwork Balloons:
An Ode to a 24hr Blood Pressure Monitor

Regular as a clockwork balloon,
The huff-puffing signifier of health,
Fitted by surprise, on a Monday afternoon,
Beeps away with no pretention of stealth,
All to prove a point we already know.

Not like there was any choice in the matter...

Irregularities in my own ticking cocoon,
Belie an unseen hand chipping away,
Dancing along to her own mad tune,
Silently plotting (clotting?!) day on day,
While tomorrow's rhythm remains a mystery.

Rolling with a fait accompli accompaniment...

Set by the Watchmaker, in flesh was hewn,
Magnificent singularities of mortal coil,
That fight, by sun and star and moon,
Inevitability, routine, the endless toil,
Always and on until there are no more.

It would have been nice to have a warning...

Ode To Insanity
Concocted On A Fridge
One Midsummer Morning
(Sometime in the early 2000s!)

I could use milk
on our raw sausage.
Yet I elaborate in silk
on incubated music and
I never dress in a beautiful human whale!

I am as though he smells:
like a sweet girl when
strangely asleep under Hell's
hot honey at the library
as the insane go into the oven.

He seems like a dog
with barely a nose to see!
As I walked, I realised (as dead parrots)
that life is represented
but the unstoppable love of pigeon pie...

All this happened
as ancient wet skin and tongues
excite the sporty petals,
while black magic inspires frantic apparatus
for a villain's sordid poetry.

Restless Legs
22.2.22

I cannot sleep.
My nerves are full of spiders,
that crawl beneath my skin
where flesh meets bone.

They flex infernal limbs.
A sudden painless agony
permeates the tissues
to wrench me from dreams.

Spinning webs hold fast.
Keeping me in a perpetual
half-waking, half-sleeping
half-life that never ends.

Something To Get Me Through The Day
9.3.22

I don't feel right this morning.

I can't precisely put my finger on it,
it's a strange sensation.

Remoteness and detachment from my surroundings,
beautiful and varied as they are;
Numbness in the face of *all* external stimuli,
not even a cold shower could shake me;
Dread that quite literally is attached to nothing,
it's just there, without form;
Confusion and disorientation and a simple question -
what the everlasting fuck is wrong with me?!

I'm sorry for swearing at a time like this.

(No I'm not, it just seems like that's
the right thing to say…)

Weirdest thing about all this, though,
is that fundamentally I am actually happy right now!
Run-of-the-mill stresses and routines
are simply mundane, ordinary – tedious;

Meanwhile I'm gearing up gradually to a new chapter,
exciting times lie ahead to occupy my headspace;
Leaving for pastures new, I will soon be away from here
and away from tethers that hold me down...

Though I know that the grass isn't always greener...

But then, even when the grass is the same
at least it isn't covered in dog shit.

I know it must seem like it to an outside observer,
but I'm not just feeling sorry for myself;
Actually I'm feeling sorry for a lot of people
and for a lot of things that I can't do;
None of this is in my control and I accept that,
but sometimes that's part of the problem;
Frustration at my own limitations is ironic,
because it just makes the limits all the more frustrating!

I'll be fine and I'll get through it, I always do.

Knowing this doesn't always help in the moment,
but at least it's something to get me through the day.

At The Edge of Silence
17.10.2021

Sometimes my mind confiscates the ability to speak.

Noises rattle, a single penny in a vast tin-can,
like thoughts broadcast into the void of space.

Unintentionally I withdraw deep deep into my shell,
away from the very soul who has the power

to bring me back from the edge.

I Can Feel The Blood
14.3.22

I can feel the blood
in my veins –
a life force,
literally pulsating,
that represents the border
between life and… not.

It calls to me
with a deep crimson scream
begging for release,
demanding a sacrifice
paid in surgical steel
… or rusty pins…

Like an Eldritch horror,
summoned from the depths
of mind-sick worshippers;
It seeks to rise,
claiming its hold
over all it surveys.

I Don't Know What Will Get Me
16.8.20

I don't know what will get me,
When the repo comes to call.
Maybe a bullet,
Stray shrapnel,
Or double-edged sword.
Unlikely, all things considered,
But not impossible.

I don't know who will take me,
Whether He or Her or Them.
A snapped ladder,
Car crash,
A bigot with a flick-knife?
Maybe. Though I try to be safe,
Follow the rules, sort of.

I don't know what they think of me,
The nameless 'They' of legend.
Tragic hero,
Abomination
Gatsby-esque mystery.
Honestly, I don't actually care,
So long as I keep myself.

Elegy for Decay
18.8.21

Sometimes I feel
like I'm just writing poetry
for a world that's dying.

Not today, not tomorrow,
perhaps not even when
you are reading this.

Because it doesn't go like that.
It ended a while ago.
While no one noticed.

A hundred thousand yesterdays,
written in terrestrial tremoring,
counted down to Zero Dawn.

Meanwhile a hundred thousand tomorrows
start oscillating spinelessly
for infinity.

Universal expansions mirror
abstract absolution that waits
for every living thing;

Black-hole vortices, blistering,
find nothing to consume
beyond themselves

and their own gravity wells
of self-entitled significance
granted by no one.

Apocalypse now sits uncomfortably
with armchair socialists
and wannabe fascistas;

They think it's all about them
imposing morality on an
indifferent future,

 but the finality of the present
holds them in contempt
banishing them from the courtroom.

Inexorably, interminably,
like a performative internment
we watch the tic tic tokking

of global events that swipe left
on a brand new device
that isn't ours.

Much like the passage of time,
progressive and constant,
yet definitive and subjective;

Working constantly day on day
off against tidal waves of
simultaneous pressure,

unrelenting, destructive and natural,
unavoidable, disruptive… but neutral
in the face of expectations.

Paths not taken lead to the same place,
when examined under a
miopic man-made microscope.

In the end, that's the problem:
poetry facilitates and reveals the
expression of internal truths,

meanwhile I am caught in between,
my truth, universal truth, false truth,
kaleidoscopic ongoing reflections

through a looking glass of silver,
smokey purple obsidian.
Beautiful. Cold. Forever.

Words Fail Me
8.9.21

For Avril Flower, a dear friend taken too suddenly
and too soon at the age of 31.

Words fail me.
Sometimes the silent memories
say it best;
They need only to be,
while you need only to rest.

You Aren't The Only One

There comes a time when every word,
And every thought,
Every sight,
Tumbles like territorial track-marks.
Proving the lie,
Masking truth,
Hiding behind crimson curtains.
Laced with fear…
Bitter aftertaste…
And all for a monthly check of worth,
A weekly chore,
The daily chum.
Edging gradually towards oblivion.

Acknowledgements

I want to keep this fairly simple, so here goes:

Thanks must first go to my wife Helen, without whom this work would not be possible. Her support and 'second pair of eyes' has been invaluable in the creation of this work and her love has kept me going.

My following on Tiktok deserves a huge portion of gratitude for the support and encouragement I have received from them – you guys are awesome!

Several people were my 'pre-alpha' readers while I was putting this collection together and their advice helped to shape the book you now hold in your hands. In no particular order, Elizabeth Biggs, Catherine Rose Hailsone, Helen Guy, Charlotte Dommett, Christina Taylor and, of course, Helen.

Trevor and Colin, if you ever read this, you know who you are and you know what you have done for me. Thank you from the bottom of my heart.

Don't let me forget my family, particularly my mum Brenda and my uncle John who have supported me and my writing in so many different ways throughout my life.

Finally, I would like to thank my dad, Richard Foster. You are here in my words, you are present in my thoughts, today and every day. Though you will never read this, I know that you would be proud.

Oh:
AND THANK YOU FOR READING! :D x

About the Author

Aisla Houghton-Foster (She/Her) is a 31 year old queer poet and author from sunny Glasgow, Scotland. She has lived all over the country, from the Isle of Mull, to Perthshire, to York and now currently lives in Liverpool with her wife Helen, bichon frise Ragnar and degu Caprica.

Aisla came out as transgender in 2018 and has since gone on to be a vocal advocate for trans rights and an active member in the trans community of Liverpool. She is immensely proud of her transition and hopes that, through her writing, she can help to normalise and celebrate trans lives.

When not writing, Aisla works within education as student support for university students, and can also be found in various nooks reading science-fiction or else snuggled in front of the her PS5 with a good game or TV show blaring away.

Website: ahfwrites.com

Follow Aisla on Tiktok, twitter and Instagram at:
@ahf.writes